YOU MAKE ME...

Illustrations by Kate Cooper

summersdale

YOU MAKE ME...

An Hachette UK Company
www.hachette.co.uk

Summersdale Publishers Ltd
Part of Octopus Publishing Group Limited
Carmelite House
50 Victoria Embankment
LONDON
EC4Y 0DZ
UK

www.summersdale.com

Printed and bound in China

ISBN: 978-1-78783-006-6

Substantial discounts on bulk quantities of Summersdale books are available to corporations, professional associations and other organizations. For details contact general enquiries: telephone: +44 (0) 1243 771107 or email: enquiries@summersdale.com.

TO ....

FROM.............................

YOU MAKE ME
SMILE

YOU MAKE ME
LAUGH

YOU MAKE ME
FEEL INSPIRED

YOU MAKE ME
BRAVE ENOUGH
TO DO THINGS
THAT SCARE ME

YOU MAKE ME
FEEL APPRECIATED

YOU MAKE ME
WANT TO SIT IN
THE BACK ROW
OF THE MOVIES
WITH YOU

YOU MAKE ME
WANT TO CUDDLE
YOU ALL DAY

YOU MAKE ME
FEEL ROMANTIC

YOU MAKE ME
WANT TO GO ON
NEW ADVENTURES

YOU MAKE ME
WANT TO TALK TO
YOU ALL DAY

YOU MAKE ME
FEEL CONFIDENT

YOU MAKE ME
WANT TO DANCE

YOU MAKE ME
WANT TO TRY
NEW THINGS

YOU MAKE ME
FEEL WEAK AT
THE KNEES

YOU MAKE ME
WANT TO GAZE AT
THE STARS WITH YOU

YOU MAKE ME FEEL SAFE

YOU MAKE ME
WANT TO SING

YOU MAKE ME
WANT TO SHOUT
"I LOVE YOU" FROM
THE ROOFTOPS

YOU MAKE ME
GLAD FOR
RAINY DAYS

YOU MAKE ME
WANT TO SHARE
MY FAVOURITE
THINGS WITH YOU

YOU MAKE ME UNAFRAID TO BE SILLY!

YOU MAKE ME
WANT TO CURL
UP AND WATCH
TV BOX SETS
WITH YOU

YOU MAKE ME
WANT TO KISS YOU

YOU MAKE ME
WANT TO SHARE MY
BATHS WITH YOU

YOU MAKE ME
WANT TO WRITE
YOU LOVE LETTERS

YOU MAKE ME
WANT TO BOOP
YOUR NOSE

YOU MAKE ME
GLAD TO BE ALIVE

YOU MAKE ME
WANT TO SPEND
ALL MY TIME
WITH YOU

YOU MAKE ME
FEEL LIKE I'M ON
TOP OF THE WORLD

YOU MAKE ME COMPLETE

IF YOU'RE INTERESTED IN FINDING OUT MORE ABOUT OUR BOOKS, FIND US ON FACEBOOK AT SUMMERSDALE PUBLISHERS AND FOLLOW US ON TWITTER AT @SUMMERSDALE.

WWW.SUMMERSDALE.COM